BAKING

20 TIPS TO GET YOUR BAKING DONE FASTER

PRODUCTIVITY

BY WORKING SMARTER, NOT HARDER

CHECKLIST

PLUS
BAKING
PRODUCTIVITY
PLANNER

GRACE ONYEMA

AUTHOR OF 2 TIME AMAZON BESTSELLING BOOK:
A BAKER'S GUIDE TO CONTENT MARKETING

DISCLAIMER

This book is simply for information purposes only. All information contained within this book is deemed accurate at the time of publishing. However, this is not an exhaustive treatment of the subjects and expert opinions may differ.

No guarantee of income or profit is intended by this book as many variables will affect each individual's results upon application, which might vary from the author's results.

If you wish to apply ideas contained within this book, you are taking full responsibility for your choices, actions, and results. The author will not assume responsibility for your results.

COPYRIGHT

All rights reserved.

Copyright © Grace Onyema 2020

INTRODUCTION

Hello! I believe the reason you are reading this right now is that you have decided to take a bold step towards becoming more productive with your baking, and that makes me glad. If I'm right about that, then you are in for a treat.

I was a procrastinator, super-lazy and I never seemed to get things done on time (probably like you). I could stay hours lazing around, waiting for the super-strength to get tasks done, or thinking about how much time it would cost me and sometimes end up taking orders or baking at the last minute (I call it the last-minute baking syndrome). You're also experiencing such, right?

I once had to bake a birthday cake and due to procrastination and had to complete the order around 2.30 am. Got up as early as 6 am to prepare for work and deliver the cake. By the end of the day, I was exhausted physically and mentally, had boots of migraine and it took me close to a week to recover fully. In all that time, I was simply unproductive.

Distractions, laziness, procrastination, and faulty time management and organizational skills can be detrimental to your baking productivity, which can also lead to serious consequences as you and I have probably experienced. There's no need to worry though because I'm going to share with you the tips I used in overcoming the cycle of laziness and procrastination to become super productive in my baking and personal life. Now, I have enough time to rest and get the work done as well.

MY WORKABLE CHECKLIST TO BECOMING MORE PRODUCTIVE WITH YOUR BAKING

1. Start Your Day With The Right Mindset

When you wake up every single day, your thought patterns and your mindset, in general, determines how the rest of your day would turn out. Everything begins with your mind. If you think you and your baking can become more productive, then you and your baking will become more productive.

Your thought pattern will affect your efficiency, work speed, accuracy, and productivity for the day. If you don't believe you can practice the tips listed in this book, then you won't be able to make them work for you and you shouldn't bother reading further.

You need to believe in yourself and believe you can achieve that task, which is an example of the right mindset, a mindset of positivity. Start your day with this kind of mindset and watch how it turns out.

2. Get Enough Rest At Night

You need to rest as much as you can at night because a productive baking day starts from the night before. You need to have slept enough and given your body, mind, and brain the rest it requires, for you to function efficiently during the day.

3. Wake Up With A Creative Mindset

When you wake up every day, do so with a creative mindset, as well as the intention to create beautiful and delicious treats or creating a new recipe. This would help keep you positive and productive, as you make your amazing treats.

4. Avoid Comparison

Your mind forms a sub-conscious belief through comparison that you are not good enough as a baker and may not be as good as other bakers.

Comparison kills productivity and you probably won't know when it started happening. You'll find out after a while that you can't get those tasks done anymore.

Comparison drains you of energy and clouds your mind, starting with that first negative thought that came with the comparison.

Guard your thoughts; think positive thoughts always so your mind can be productive.

5. Avoid Looking At Digital Screens Before Sleeping At Night

Stay away from your digital screens (mobile phone, laptop, etc.), at least an hour or 30 minutes before you sleep. The light from digital screens tends to stimulate our brains and keep them awake, and this isn't good for you if you are trying to get enough rest at night.

You can read a book instead or listen to music which helps the relaxation of your mind.

6. Plan Your Daily Routines

Planning your daily routines (morning, noontime, and night) instead of just letting things happen on their own daily will go a long way in making your day more productive.

Planning your daily activities makes you aware of what tasks to be carried out at a particular time, when you should be resting, etc.

7. Avoid Overloading Your Mind With Expectations

Do not overload your mind and emotions with expectations, by trying to do everything you need to do at the same time. Break up your tasks, arrange them according to priorities, and get things done at your pace so you don't get overwhelmed. Arrange your tasks according to what works best for you in other to achieve them.

There is a baking productivity planner attached at the end of this book, which will help you successfully plan your daily, weekly, or monthly activities. This planner has helped me work wonders and I'm sure it will do the same for you.

Be realistic and honest with yourself about which tasks suit you better at certain times of the day, as what works for you may be the opposite of another baker.

8. Avoid Distractions

Keep your gadgets away from your kitchen when you are baking, especially your mobile phone. Social media can wait, that message can be replied when you're done. Don't let Instagram or Facebook steal your time and productivity.

Baking in batches is also very essential, as it reduces distractions, saves you time, and keeps your baking process less stressful. Prepare your ingredients, measure them out, and get them ready for each batch of baking.

9. Take A Break and Rest

Strategic resting makes you more productive. You need to be disciplined about your resting times, stop slaving. Most bakers struggle to rest because they see resting as a waste of time, but you can't be productive when you burn out or if you're constantly exhausted.

There was a time I worked so hard on a project for two weeks without rest, by the time the project was completed, I looked like a zombie. I fell ill immediately and it took me a long time to fully recover. That was my body reacting to the excessive stress; I learned my lesson the hard way.

When it's time for you to rest, avoid doing so by watching series or movies because that would put a strain on your brain. Instead relax with a novel, play classical music, and have a cup of tea. It works magic.

Find a way to take a break from that work and REST, even if it's just for about 30 minutes twice a day. This would help relax your mind and body from all the work and make you more productive throughout the rest of the day.

10. Invest In Time Saving Tools

Baking with time-saving tools or equipment goes a long way in helping you achieve your baking goals faster. Investing in tools or service that saves you time and increase your baking capacity will, in turn, grow your bakery business, generate more profit and increase your productivity.

Are you aware that your time is the most valuable and priceless commodity you have? Well, now you know.

11. Have An Organized Bakery Layout

Your bakery layout should be well planned as this would aid the transportation of materials, baked goods, and movement. If you are a home baker, the baking space in your kitchen should be well organized as well. Mixers, baking pans, and other tools should be properly stored and easily accessible. This helps to save time and reduce unnecessary stress.

12. Set Clear Goals With The Productivity Planner

What tasks do you hope to complete faster? What are your daily or weekly goals? What would be the consequence of not meeting up with that order?

Ask yourself these questions, as this will help you properly allocate time to each activity that needs to be carried out to achieve your set goals.

13. Hire An Extra Hand

This would help you save time, reduce stress, and make your baking more productive. There are some tasks you don't have to do on your own, you can either delegate or outsource to someone else. If you try to control all aspects of your bakery business, you will be overly strained and possibly lose sight of the actual job you are supposed to do.

You don't have to be the head baker, social media marketer, graphics designer, accountant, the delivery person, and all the other stuff at the same time. You can hire a personal assistant to reduce your workload by handling social media marketing, sales, or accounting aspect, so you can take your time in baking those sweet treats with love.

14.   Always Review Your To-Do List

Reviewing your to-do list goes a long way in helping you plan your daily or weekly tasks. Some tasks shouldn't make it to your productivity planner from your to-do list. Planning your day the night before helps to prepare your tasks for the next day.

When you draw out your to-do list, take note of tasks to be outsourced, urgent tasks, not so urgent tasks, etc., so as not to take up valuable time that should be spent attending to other tasks that require your attention.

15.   Avoid Listening To Your Thoughts

Avoid listening to thoughts like "I'll do this much faster at night" or "I bake best at night" or "Maybe I should just take a short nap". Take the right path instead of taking the easy part by giving into laziness.

Whenever I get those thoughts that make me want to procrastinate on carrying out a task, I immediately look at my productivity planner and my brain resets itself. It'll help you a great deal also.

16. Do Not Neglect Your Personal Activities

Do not get so caught up in your baking that you end up forgetting your personal activities. Activities such as picking the kids up from school, cooking dinner, lunch dates, taking a walk, etc. Be sure to add them to your productivity planner or to-do list.

Don't forget to include your family in your daily activities, so you can avoid random activities popping up on your work schedule and causing distractions.

Incorporate your personal activities into your to-do list or productivity planner to achieve better productivity with your work.

17. Stick To Your Schedule

The baking productivity planner is designed in such a way that you get to punish yourself if you miss a task on your work schedule. Yes, you read that right. It is easier to create a schedule but difficult most times to stick to it. At first, it may seem hard but when you get a hang of it, it becomes easy.

Some people punish themselves for not meeting up to their tasks and I do that as well. It helps keep me in check and I never want to be punished, so I tend to get things done and fast. If it's okay for you to reward yourself for little successes, then it's okay to punish yourself for little failures too.

18. Exercise Regularly

It is very important to exercise often. Don't stick to one spot or stay in a position for long. Do some yoga, stretch your legs, dance to music, walk around your house, or bakery. Exercise works wonders for your body, mood, and health throughout the day.

19. Reward Your Successes

For every little win, you get, reward yourself with a treat. This is a very important step to becoming more productive, and it is linked to your body, mindset, and emotions.

Give yourself a treat after delivering that castle wedding cake or 2,000 cupcakes or completing an event where you baked sweet treats for 3 days straight. Celebrating small wins and successes is a great motivating factor for successful people. Just get yourself a reward that's small and significant, no need to go overboard.

Whenever I complete a major or little task, I like to indulge myself in sweet treats or ice-cream, pizza, or even get a new earring or dress.

20. Let The Process Become A Habit

Make the process a habit by repeating these tips day after day, month after month, and year after year. Even though it may take a while, it will be worth it. Also, always stay positive and have the right mindset towards this.

Now, these tips have helped me in staying super-productive and having a productive baking experience, and even though I still procrastinate and get distracted a few times, I have been able to achieve so much more daily, which wouldn't have been normally possible.

SAMPLE: TO-DO LIST

TO-DO LIST

- [ ] Inventory Check
- [ ] Baking orders
- [ ] Social media post
- [ ] House clean-up
- [ ] Reply mails/messages
- [ ] Laundry
- [ ] Customer follow-up
- [ ] Prepare a meal
- [ ] Recipe creation
- [ ]
- [ ]

SAMPLE: BAKING PRODUCTIVITY PLANNER

BAKING PRODUCTIVITY PLANNER

PHASE 1 — MORNING

TASK CHECKLIST
- TASK FROM TO-DO LIST
- PREPARATION OF INGREDIENTS
- DIVIDE BAKING INTO BATCHES

PHASE 2 — AFTERNOON

TASK CHECKLIST
- BAKING SHIFT | FIRST BATCH OF BAKING
- LUNCH | SHORT BREAK
- TASK FROM TO-DO LIST

PHASE 3 — LATE AFTERNOON

TASK CHECKLIST
- BAKING SHIFT | SECOND BATCH OF BAKING
- TEA BREAK | REST
- TASK FROM TO-DO LIST

SECRET TIPS:

- Get an accountability partner for the major tasks on your baking productivity planner.
- Attach something tangible to those tasks (e.g. money, a favorite possession, etc. I usually use money).
- Give those tasks a time frame for completion.
- Now, when you complete those tasks, you get to keep your money (or whatever you chose).
- If you don't meet up with those tasks you set, you lose your money (or whatever you chose) and it goes to your accountability partner.

This structure has helped in improving my baking productivity and I believe this will help you accomplish more baking in less time.

CONCLUSION

Baking productivity is a skill any baker can learn. A lot of bakers don't wake up being productive, but there are easy and workable tips you can use to become more productive in your baking and accomplish your daily or weekly tasks.

These tips range from having a resourceful mindset to starting your day early with a creative mindset and planning your day the night before, getting enough rest and exercising regularly, organization and time management, avoiding distractions, sticking to your schedule, and rewarding your successes. Every baker has the potential to be more productive in their baking and learning how to properly manage their time and energy makes the whole difference.

ABOUT THE AUTHOR

Grace Onyema is a Baker, Content Creator and an Author. She empowers people with all they need to become successful bakery business owners and professionals without spending a fortune.

Her passion for empowering individuals and bakery business owners with the right knowledge and skill set needed to thrive, become productive with their baking and scale-up their businesses in the industry is duly represented in the books she has written/authored.

When she isn't baking, writing or creating new recipes, you can find her reading novels, surfing the internet or making research on health and nutrition.

www.ingramcontent.com/pod-product-compliance
Lightning Source LLC
Chambersburg PA
CBHW050328220526
45465CB00005B/2180